WHAT IS EROSION?

BY FRANCES NAGLE

Gareth Stevens
PUBLISHING

CRASH COURSE

Please visit our website, www.garethstevens.com. For a free color catalog of all our high-quality books, call toll free 1-800-542-2595 or fax 1-877-542-2596.

Library of Congress Cataloging-in-Publication Data

Names: Nagle, Frances, 1959-
Title: What is erosion? / Frances Nagle.
Description: New York : Gareth Stevens Publishing, [2018] | Series: A look at Earth's rocks | Includes index.
Identifiers: LCCN 2016039341| ISBN 9781482460155 (pbk. book) | ISBN 9781482460162 (6 pack) | ISBN 9781482460179 (library bound book)
Subjects: LCSH: Erosion--Juvenile literature.
Classification: LCC QE571 .N24 2018 | DDC 551.3/02--dc23
LC record available at https://lccn.loc.gov/2016039341

First Edition

Published in 2018 by
Gareth Stevens Publishing
111 East 14th Street, Suite 349
New York, NY 10003

Copyright © 2018 Gareth Stevens Publishing

Designer: Samantha DeMartin
Editor: Kristen Nelson

Photo credits: Series background winnond/Shutterstock.com; caption box Edhar Shvets/Shutterstock.com; cover, p. 1 Josemaria Toscano/Shutterstock.com; p. 5 BMJ/Shutterstock.com; p. 7 Cahir Davitt/Getty Images; p. 9 Oleg_Mit/Shutterstock.com; p. 11 Laura Livre/EyeEm/Getty Images; p. 13 Jarrod Blaesing/EyeEm/Getty Images; p. 15 GRCO Images/Shutterstock.com; p. 17 Svetlana Foote/Shutterstock.com; p. 19 AGF/Universal Images Group/Getty Images; p. 21 Nerdist72/Shutterstock.com; p. 23 silky/Shutterstock.com; p. 25 ValeryRuta/Shutterstock.com; p. 27 Dan Schreiber/Shutterstock.com; p. 29 Silvia Otte/Getty Images; p. 30 (water) Humannet/Shutterstock.com; p. 30 (people) Jacob Lund/Shutterstock.com; p. 30 (ice) Bernhard Staehli/Shutterstock.com; p. 30 (gravity) Olaf Speier/Shutterstock.com; p. 30 (wind) jukurae/Shutterstock.com.

Printed in China

CPSIA compliance information: Batch #CS17GS: For further information contact Gareth Stevens, New York, New York at 1-800-542-2595.

CONTENTS

Words in the glossary appear in **bold** type the first time they are used in the text.

ROCK ON THE MOVE

Have you ever seen stones wash up on the beach? Maybe you've seen dry soil fly into the air when the wind kicks up. Rocks and sediment are on the move all the time. This **process** is called erosion.

MAKE THE GRADE

Sediment is matter, such as stones and sand, that's carried onto land or into the water by wind, water, or land movement.

WEARING DOWN

Weathering often occurs before erosion happens. Weathering is the breakdown of rocks into sediment. **Physical** weathering, such as when wind blows matter at a rock and chips pieces away, changes the size or shape of a rock.

MAKE THE GRADE

Another way physical weathering may occur is when water flows into a rock, freezes, and causes it to crack.

7

Chemical weathering is the addition of new matter, such as **minerals** or gases, which causes a rock to break down or its makeup to change. Rain is a common way chemical weathering happens. Rainwater mixes with matter and flows over and into rocks.

MAKE THE GRADE

A rock's mineral makeup and the average weather of an area play a part in how and when weathering occurs.

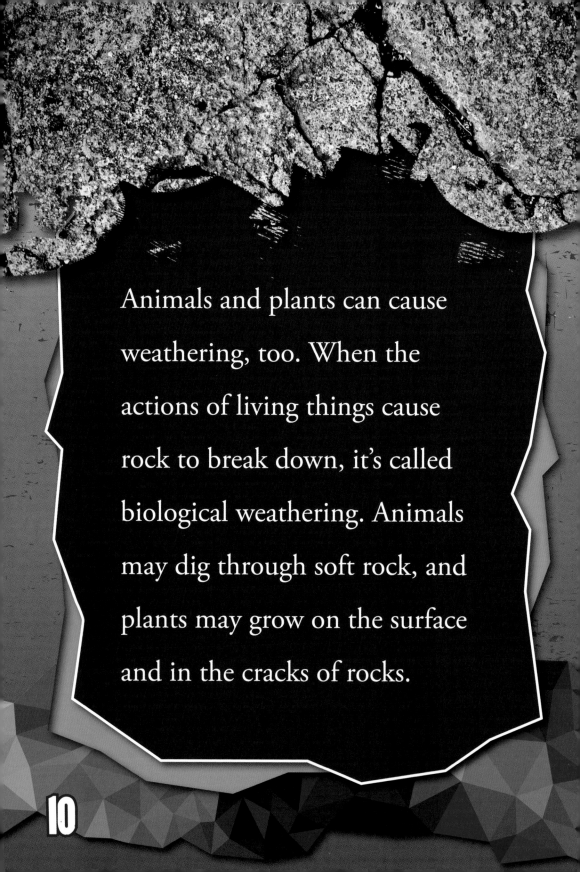

Animals and plants can cause weathering, too. When the actions of living things cause rock to break down, it's called biological weathering. Animals may dig through soft rock, and plants may grow on the surface and in the cracks of rocks.

MAKE THE GRADE

Some kinds of bacteria make chemicals
that cause rock to break down.

CARRIED AWAY

After weathering occurs, the sediment it creates may stay put. However, it's often moved and **deposited** in a new place. The process of sediment moving away from where it was created is called erosion.

MAKE THE GRADE

Erosion can happen quickly or slowly. It may happen soon after weathering creates sediment. Or sediment can move after staying in one place for years!

13

There are many natural ways erosion occurs. Gravity, or the force that pulls everything toward Earth's center, is one major **agent** of erosion. It can cause rocks to roll slowly downhill. It can also cause rockslides, when lots of rocks fall quickly!

MAKE THE GRADE

You can be an agent of erosion! Anytime you pick up and throw a rock or kick some sand around, you're causing erosion.

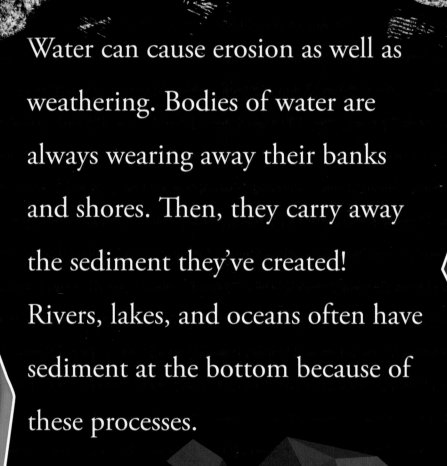

Water can cause erosion as well as weathering. Bodies of water are always wearing away their banks and shores. Then, they carry away the sediment they've created! Rivers, lakes, and oceans often have sediment at the bottom because of these processes.

MAKE THE GRADE

Rain can cause erosion by carrying soil and other matter as it flows downhill, into bodies of water, and down drains.

17

Wind is an agent of erosion, too. It blows around loose sand, soil, and other sediment. As wind moves some sediment, it creates even more sediment! Sediment can wear away mountains and landforms as the wind carries it.

MAKE THE GRADE

Huge sheets of ice called glaciers can cause erosion. They travel slowly, pushing and dragging sediment as they move.

19

THE ROCK CYCLE

Erosion is a step in the rock cycle, a scientific model that explains how rock breaks down and re-forms on Earth. The cycle shows that weathering and erosion are part of the creation of almost all the rock on our planet!

MAKE THE GRADE

The rock cycle shows the three main types of rock: **igneous** rock, **metamorphic** rock, and **sedimentary** rock.

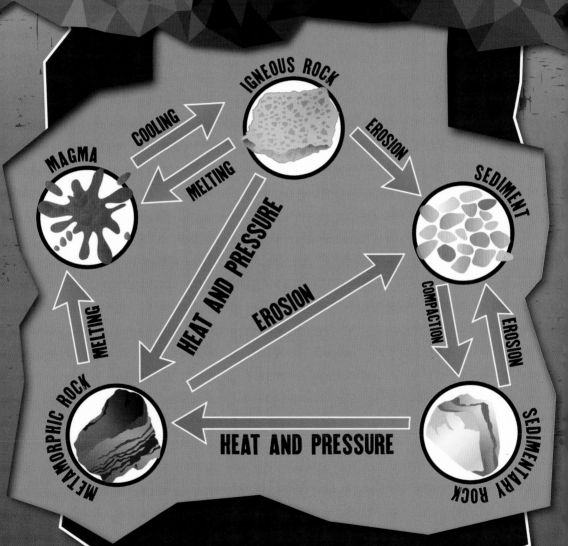

WONDERS OF EROSION

Some of the world's natural wonders have formed because of erosion. The Grand Canyon is one of them! Millions of years ago, the flow of the Colorado River began to weather and erode rock to create this beautiful landform.

MAKE THE GRADE

The natural agents of erosion work together to move sediment.

Erosion is part of waterfall formation, too! Water flows over **layers** of hard and soft rock. The softer rock breaks down and erodes more quickly than the harder rock. The water's path gets steeper as the rock erodes at different speeds.

MAKE THE GRADE

Erosion doesn't stop once people think a landform is beautiful! Wind, water, gravity, and other agents of erosion continue to move sediment, changing the land over time.

CAUSING HARM?

Erosion is an important part of the rock cycle, but it can be a problem, too. Too much rain can start mudslides. Rock loosened by weathering can be pulled down by gravity in landslides and rockslides. All these can **damage** cars and homes.

MAKE THE GRADE

When it's dry, the wind can carry needed soil away from farms. This harms crops.

Trees and plants help hold the soil in place. Clearing large areas to build can increase erosion that harms people. Soil and other matter can get into drinking water. Extra dust in the air because of erosion can also spread illnesses!

MAKE THE GRADE

Water carries sediment as it moves over land, but it also may mix with chemicals and waste. If people drink these, they'll get sick!

AGENTS OF EROSION

PEOPLE

GRAVITY

WIND

ICE

WATER

GLOSSARY

agent: something that produces an effect

chemical: having to do with matter that can be mixed with other matter to cause changes. Also, the matter itself.

damage: to cause harm

deposit: to let fall or sink

igneous: having to do with the rock that forms when hot, liquid rock from within Earth rises and cools

layer: one thickness of something lying over or under another

metamorphic: having to do with rock that has been changed by temperature, pressure, or other natural forces

mineral: matter in the ground that forms rocks

physical: having to do with matter

process: a natural continuing action

sedimentary: having to do with the rock that forms when sand, stones, and other matter are pressed together over a long time

FOR MORE INFORMATION

BOOKS

Brannon, Cecelia H. *A Look at Erosion and Weathering.* New York, NY: Enslow Publishing, 2016.

Maurer, Daniel D. *Do You Really Want to Create a Mudslide? A Book About Erosion.* Mankato, MN: Amicus, 2017.

WEBSITES

Earth Science for Kids: Erosion
ducksters.com/science/earth_science/erosion.php
Review even more information about erosion here.

Rock Cycle
dkfindout.com/us/earth/rock-cycle/
Check out an interactive diagram of the rock cycle.

INDEX